Spring Harvest
Bible Workbook

MOSES

Friend of God

Elizabeth McQuoid

Series editor for Bible character workbooks – Ian Coffey

LIFESTYLE

Equipping the Church for action

Copyright © 2003 Elizabeth McQuoid

First published in 2003 Spring Harvest Publishing Division and Authentic Lifestyle

09 08 07 06 05 04 03   7 6 5 4 3 2 1

Authentic Lifestyle is an imprint of Authentic Media

PO Box 300, Carlisle, Cumbria, CA3 0QS, UK

and Box 1047, Waynesboro, GA 30830-2047, USA

www.paternoster-publishing.com

British Library Cataloguing in Publication Data

A catalogue record for this book is available from the British Library

ISBN 1-85078-519-8

Typeset by Spring Harvest
Cover design by Diane Bainbridge
Printed in Great Britain by Bell and Bain Ltd., Glasgow

CONTENTS

ABOUT THIS BOOK

The aim of this study guide is look at the life and character of Moses. We'll follow his personal journey from Pharaoh's palace to the dark days in the desert. By stepping back into the world of the Old Testament we'll face the same challenges Moses did – to see the big picture of God's plan for the world and to play our part in it.

This book is written primarily for a group situation, but can easily be used by individuals who want to study the life of Moses. It can be used in a variety of contexts, so it is perhaps helpful to spell out the assumptions that we have made about the groups that will use it. These can have a variety of names – homegroups, Bible study groups, cell groups – we've used housegroup as the generic term.

▶ The emphasis of the studies will be on the application of the Bible. Group members will not just learn facts, but will be encouraged to think 'How does this apply to me? What change does it require of me? What incidents or situations in my life is this relevant to?'
▶ Housegroups can encourage honesty and make space for questions and doubts. The aim of the studies is not to find the 'right answer', but to help members understand the Bible by working through their questions. The Christian faith throws up paradoxes. Events in people's lives may make particular verses difficult to understand. The housegroup should be a safe place to express these concerns.
▶ Housegroups can give opportunities for deep friendships to develop. Group members will be encouraged to talk about their experiences, feelings, questions, hopes and fears. They will be able to offer one another pastoral support and to get involved in each other's lives.
▶ There is a difference between being a collection of individuals who happen to meet together every Wednesday and being an effective group who bounce ideas off each other, spark inspiration and creativity, pooling their talents and resources to create solutions together: one whose whole is definitely greater than the sum of its parts. The process of working through these studies will encourage healthy group dynamics.

Space is given for you to write answers, comments, questions and thoughts. This book will not tell you what to think, but will help you discover the truth of God's word through thinking, discussing, praying and listening.

FOR GROUP MEMBERS

▶ You will probably get more out of the study if you spend some time during the week reading the passage and thinking about the questions. Make a note of anything you don't understand.

▶ Pray that God will help you to understand the passage and show you how to apply it. Pray for other members in the group too, that they will find the study helpful.

▶ Be willing to take part in the discussions. The leader of the group is not there as an expert with all the answers. They will want everyone to get involved and share their thoughts and opinions.

▶ However, don't dominate the group! If you are aware that you are saying a lot, make space for others to contribute. Be sensitive to other group members and aim to be encouraging. If you disagree with someone, say so but without putting down their contribution.

FOR INDIVIDUALS

▶ Although this book is written with a group in mind, it can also be easily used by individuals. You obviously won't be able to do the group activities suggested, but you can consider how you would answer the questions and write your thoughts in the space provided.

▶ You may find it helpful to talk to a prayer partner about what you have learnt, and ask them to pray for you as you try and apply what you are learning to your life.

▶ The New International Version of the text is printed in the book. If you use a different version, then read from your own Bible as well.

INTRODUCTION TO MOSES

The diary Moses kept for the children of Israel, recorded in the first five books of the Bible, reads like an epic. But of all of the events we read about, the Exodus from Egypt stands out above the rest. This would be the one story all Jewish children would know about. It was even re-enacted every Passover so that none of the Israelites would forget how costly their escape from Egypt was. This rescue plan was sealed with the blood of a lamb. This was a picture pointing forwards towards the death of another spotless lamb, Jesus Christ, God's son. Jesus was God's rescue package, not only for the Israelites but for the whole world.

Given that the Exodus was such an important mission, we could be forgiven for asking why it was entrusted to a murderer exiled in the desert. Yet on closer inspection, we see that God had been preparing Moses for this task from birth. His training ground had been the opulence of Pharaoh's palace as well as the loneliness of the desert. In time, this stuttering shepherd became a politician and military strategist, an accomplished writer, a judge and legal expert. The scale of God's rescue plan was incredible but that God would chose to do all this through the life of one man was truly amazing. As it turned out, what God would do in Moses' life was just as important as the mission he would carry out though him.

Through Moses' life we can see a man being prepared by God for service, battling with his own temptations and weaknesses and facing critical opposition. We can identify with his feelings of inadequacy, his times in the wilderness and his frustrations in God's service. And yet this Old Testament hero encourages us that the great 'I AM' can take our backgrounds and failures and use them as part of his plan. Moses' experience reminds us that flawed men and women can still meet with the Living God, can still see and radiate his glory. Like Moses, we have a part to play in God's great salvation plan for the world. Are we listening for God's call? Are we willing to be obedient whatever the cost?

THE EARLY YEARS
GOD SHAPES HIS SERVANT FOR FUTURE SERVICE

 AIM: To see how our lives can be used by God as part of his mission

Hindsight is a useful commodity, isn't it? Often it's only with hindsight that we can make sense of all that happens in our lives. But it helps to realise that through all the highs and lows of life, God can be shaping us into the people he wants us to be and preparing us for his service.

Now a man of the house of Levi married a Levite woman, and she became pregnant and gave birth to a son. When she saw that he was a fine child, she hid him for three months. But when she could hide him no longer, she got a papyrus basket for him and coated it with tar and pitch. Then she placed the child in it and put it among the reeds along the bank of the Nile. His sister stood at a distance to see what would happen to him.

Then Pharaoh's daughter went down to the Nile to bathe, and her attendants were walking along the riverbank. She saw the basket among the reeds and sent her slave girl to get it. She opened it and saw the baby. He was crying, and she felt sorry for him. 'This is one of the Hebrew babies,' she said.

Then his sister asked Pharaoh's daughter, 'Shall I go and get one of the Hebrew women to nurse the baby for you?'

'Yes, go,' she answered. And the girl went and got the baby's mother.

Exodus 2:1–8

TO SET THE SCENE
Get to know the others in your group by sharing how an event, experience or circumstance in your background has helped shape the person you are today. Explain the experience and how it impacted you. How did it shape your behaviour, your attitudes and how you perceive the world?

Read Exodus 2–3:1

1 Brainstorm together the key elements of God's mission in the world. What is the big picture? What is God most concerned to do with humanity throughout history?

2 Exodus gives us an historical slice of God's rescue mission. Scan back over Exodus 1 – why did Israel need rescuing?

3 In 2:1–11, how does the writer prepare us for Moses playing a significant part in God's rescue package of the Israelites?

4 Divide your group into three teams. Have one team focus on the palace years (Ex. 2: 1–10); the second team on Moses' murder of the Egyptian (Ex. 2:11–15); and the third team the desert wanderings (Ex. 2:16–3:1). Have each team look at:

    a) The experiences Moses had which would help him face Pharaoh and lead the Exodus.
    b) What strengths emerged which God would use?
    c) What weaknesses emerged for which God would later compensate?

When you have had time to brainstorm together in teams, report your findings back to the whole group.

5 Moses was separated from his family when he was young and later had to flee to the desert. These can't have been pleasant experiences. How has God used apparently negative experiences in your life for his good?

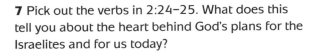

6 Read Acts 7:23–29. Clearly God would use Moses to rescue the Israelites but not just yet. What have you learnt about the importance of God's timing in carrying out his plans?

7 Pick out the verbs in 2:24–25. What does this tell you about the heart behind God's plans for the Israelites and for us today?

8 Now think about these issues of background and experience with regard to your own life:

    a) In twos, explain what kind of Christian service/ministry you are currently involved in.

    b) What factors from your background prepared you for this role?

    c) What strengths and interests have you cultivated for this role?

    d) Is there any other ministry/service your gifts, interests and past experience would point you to?

HOW DOES THIS

?

APPLY TO ME

9 How does it feel to see your service for God as part of his whole mission for the world?

Rabbi Zusya ... said 'When I stand before God before God I will not be asked "Why were you not Moses?" but "Why were you not Zusya?"'

John Glass

WORSHIP

We can be part of God's plan just like Moses was. But the central hero in God's plan was Christ. Just as the events in our past can shape us, so the events in Christ's past can shape us too. Amazingly the power of the cross can make us more like Christ! Spend time committing yourself to being part of God's mission. Then, as a group, thank God that Jesus fulfilled his role in this mission. Praise God for Christ's work on our behalf, the passions and concerns that spurred him on and those things that made him uniquely suited to be the Saviour of the world.

FOR NEXT WEEK

Spend some time doing a spiritual SWOT analysis (Strengths, Weaknesses, Opportunities, and Threats).

Think through your strengths – your character strengths and the spiritual gifts you have been given; weaknesses – the weaknesses in your character and the areas where you lack gifting; opportunities – how will you maximise the gifts you've been given, what opportunities for service should you look for, where do you think God may be guiding you; threats – what can you see standing in the way of you becoming the person God has in mind, how can you avoid these traps?

This exercise may help you find the niche God has been specially preparing you for!

THE BURNING BUSH
GOD CALLS A SHEPHERD TO LEAD HIS FLOCK

AIM: To live for God wholeheartedly in the specific context he has planned for us

Many books have been written to help Christians discover their 'calling' because we each have a God-given desire to invest our lives in something significant. Moses' encounter at the burning bush reminds us that God is primarily interested in holiness – our wholehearted commitment to him. The context of where we serve him is an important but secondary matter.

> *Now Moses was tending the flock of Jethro his father-in-law, the priest of Midian, and he led the flock to the far side of the desert and came to Horeb, the mountain of God. There the angel of the Lord appeared to him in flames of fire from within a bush. Moses saw that though the bush was on fire it did not burn up. So Moses thought 'I will go over and see this strange sight – why the bush does not burn up.'*
>
> *When the Lord saw that he had gone over to look, God called to him from within the bush, 'Moses! Moses!'*
>
> *And Moses said, 'Here I am,'*
>
> *'Do not come any closer,' God said. 'Take off your sandals, for the place where you're standing is holy ground.' Then he said 'I am the God of your father, the God of Abraham, the God of Isaac and the God of Jacob.' At this Moses hid his face, because he was afraid to look at God.*

Exodus 3:1–6

TO SET THE SCENE
Discuss together what has given you the greatest buzz in life; what topic would keep you up all night talking, what issue would you really like the opportunity to tackle? You may be surprised at some people's answers but often our passions and interests give us an idea what God has specifically designed us for.

Read Exodus 3:1–4:17

1 Moses demonstrated his holiness in a practical way by taking off his sandals (3:5). How would you describe 'holiness' and how do we demonstrate it today?

> *Earth's crammed with heaven,*
> *And every common bush afire with God;*
> *But only he who sees takes off his shoes...*
> **Elizabeth Barrett Browning**

2 How do you feel knowing that living for God gives every part of your life value and significance?

> *Calling is not about 'Christian Ministry', but about 'living for the praise and glory of the Lord and serving God's purpose in every context of life.'*
> **Jani Rubery**

We can't be holy in a vacuum and God 'calls' each of us to live for him in a particular context. At the burning bush, God introduced Moses to his part in the divine plan – and like many of us, he didn't feel up to the job!

WHAT DOES SEARCH THE BIBLE SAY? **3** Look at 3:6,15,16 and 4:5. God describes himself as the God of Abraham, Isaac and Jacob, the Old Testament patriarchs. Why do you think this introduction would be significant for Moses and for the Israelites?

4 Imagine yourself at the Oscar ceremony presenting the award for best leading actor. Who would you choose for the burning bush scene? Explain your answer by referring to specific verses in the passage.

5 Brainstorm what the name of God in 3:14 tells us about his character. Write your answers on a sheet of A4 paper or a flipchart.

6 In twos, share with each other what your own particular calling is – it could be to raise a family, to work in the public sector, to minister to Muslims etc. Spend time praying for each other and your areas of service for God.

7 How do your answers to questions 3 to 5 make you feel when you think of your own particular calling?

8 How does God's response to Moses' questioning of his call (Ex. 3:11–15 and 4:1–17) put your own anxieties to rest?

9 Is God calling you to something new and challenging? Are you willing to be obedient whatever the cost?

God's calling is the key to igniting a passion for the deepest growth and highest heroism in life.

Os Guinness

WORSHIP

Put the flipchart or A4 sheet with your answers to question 5 into the centre of the room. Use these character qualities of God to focus your worship. Perhaps play a tape or CD of a song about God's character or his names. Then cut the sheet of paper up, so that each person has a slip of paper with a character trait of God on. On the back of the piece of paper write down your fears and what is holding you back from total obedience to God. As you face these issues this week, focus instead on the character of God written on your slip of paper. Let God empower your service this week.

FURTHER STUDY

Os Guinness – *The Call*, published by Spring Harvest

Jani Rubery – *More than a Job*, published by Spring Harvest

FOR NEXT WEEK

Some of us are not sure what specific context God wants us to serve him in. Often the particulars of our 'calling' change over time and we need to keep re-evaluating where God wants us to be. Jani Rubery, in *More than a Job*, suggests five practical steps you could put into practice this week to begin this search.

▶ Pray and fast to help you focus
▶ Listen to God
▶ Understand yourself – your gifts, passions, values, skills
▶ Talk to others to confirm or re-evaluate your findings
▶ Open doors to explore options

ACTIVITY PAGE

Christians may talk about God 'calling' them to a particular ministry but in church we don't often talk about how we can discover our calling or be sure of it. How would you advise the following people about their 'calling'? Think in terms of their primary calling to be holy and their secondary calling to serve God in the specific context he has prepared them for:

▶ A young mother struggling at home with her three toddlers. She can't get very involved in church life and misses the stimulus of outside work.

▶ A lay preacher who feels very fulfilled every Sunday he preaches but equally very depressed when he doesn't have any involvement in the church service.

▶ Someone juggling family life, church and work but with no certainty that God has specifically 'called' them into the job/roles they are now occupying. They are hesitant about how to go about discovering their true 'calling'.

OUT OF EGYPT
GOD'S PROMISE OF LIBERATION IS FULFILLED

AIM: To remember that God is always faithful to us, he keeps his promises

How many times have you promised someone something and then failed to deliver? With the hectic pace of life and constant demands on our time, it is often hard to honour the commitments we make. In contrast, God always keeps his promises. His promise to the Israelites and to us is freedom so that we can serve him wholeheartedly.

> *God also said to Moses, 'I am the Lord. I appeared to Abraham, to Isaac and to Jacob as God Almighty, but by my name the Lord I did not make myself known to them. I also established my covenant with them to give them the land of Canaan, where they lived as aliens. Moreover, I have heard the groaning of the Israelites, whom the Egyptians are enslaving, and I have remembered my covenant.*
>
> *Therefore say to the Israelites: 'I am the Lord, and I will bring you out from under the yoke of the Egyptians. I will free you from being slaves to them, and I will redeem you with an outstretched arm and with mighty acts of judgement. I will take you as my own people, and I will be your God. Then you will know that I am the Lord your God, who brought you out from under the yoke of the Egyptians. And I will bring you to the land I swore with uplifted hand to give to Abraham, to Isaac and to Jacob. I will give it to you as a possession. I am the Lord.'*

Exodus 6:2–8

TO SET THE SCENE
Have a few people in the group share a promise they made to someone. It could be something relatively minor or more significant. Can the other group members tell which person kept their promise and who didn't? Discuss from your experience the reasons why people break promises.

Read Exodus 4:29–5:2, 5:19–6:12, 12:21–28, 31–36

1 God's promise to free the Israelites was opposed by Pharaoh, so God sent plagues on the land. Scan chapters 7–11. What plagues did God send?

2 Why did God stop the plagues each time Moses asked him to do so, when he knew that Pharaoh would keep on resisting him?

3 On one level the contest between Moses and Pharaoh was a spiritual one. What evidence can you find that a spiritual battle was going on?

APPLY THIS TO **4** Jesus decisively defeated the power of Satan on the cross so what role do individual Christians and the church have in MY CHURCH spiritual warfare?

5 God's determination to fulfil his promise to liberate his people was demonstrated in the Passover feast (12:1–11). What did the various elements symbolise:

- ▶ The lamb
- ▶ The blood
- ▶ The bitter herbs
- ▶ The bread without yeast

ENGAGING WITH **6** The liberation of people from Satan's grip is still God's mission. In what ways does slavery exist today? Think about your THE WORLD answer in terms of Christians and non-Christians.

God is the champion of the poor and those pushed to the margins of life. God is the one who liberates them from the Pharaohs of this world.

Terence Fretheim

WHAT DOES SEARCH THE BIBLE SAY?

7 As it turned out, the fulfilment of God's promise was even better than the Israelites expected. Look at 12:31–36 to explain why.

HOW DOES THIS APPLY TO ME

8 What other promises has God given in the Bible? Has this passage encouraged you to trust God more?

WORSHIP

God's desire for us to be free is most clearly demonstrated on the cross. The Passover was a forerunner to our communion service where we remember Jesus' death for us. The blood of Jesus cleanses us from the power of sin and frees us from its penalty. Take time to share communion, saying as you serve the elements to one another 'The body/blood of Christ has set you free.'

FURTHER STUDY

If you are interested in exploring the issue of freedom in Christ further, try reading Dr Neil T. Anderson's book *Bondage Breaker*. If you want to find out how you can be involved in freeing people from the many forms of contemporary slavery, contact your local Evangelical Alliance office to find out about the projects that are running in your area or contact Christian Solidarity Worldwide.

FOR NEXT WEEK

Throughout this account, God told Moses to say to Pharaoh, 'Let my people go that they may worship me.' That is God's desire for us – that we be free to worship him alone. Jesus has freed us from sin's power but often we let it continue to dominate us. Do you feel enslaved? Is there an area of your life where Satan rather than God is in control? You could be enslaved by guilt or fear, anxiety about work, or bitterness because of an unanswered prayer. Confess these things to the Lord. Meet up with a friend this week and pray for each other that you won't be slaves to sin but slaves to righteousness.

CROSSING THE RED SEA
AGAINST ALL THE ODDS GOD SAVES HIS PEOPLE

AIM: To see God's hand in our salvation and subsequent freedom

We don't like to think of ourselves as helpless or dependent, but for our salvation we are completely dependent on God's intervention. God masterminded the rescue plan for humanity and is the initiator at each stage – for the children of Israel in the Exodus and for us in the cross.

> Then the Lord said to Moses, 'Stretch out your hand over the sea so that the waters may flow back over the Egyptians and their chariots and their horsemen.' Moses stretched out his hand over the sea, and at daybreak the sea went back to its place. The Egyptians were fleeing toward it, and the Lord swept them into the sea. The water flowed back and covered the chariots and horsemen – the entire army of Pharaoh that had followed the Israelites into the sea. Not one of them survived.
>
> But the Israelites went through the sea on dry ground, with a wall of water on their right and on their left. That day the Lord saved Israel from the hands of the Egyptians, and Israel saw the Egyptians lying dead on the shore. And when the Israelites saw the great power the Lord displayed against the Egyptians, the people feared the Lord and put their trust in him and Moses his servant.
>
> ***Exodus 14:26–31***

TO SET THE SCENE
Describe how you became a Christian –

▶ Was it more of a process or an event?
▶ Was it helped or hindered by your background?
▶ Was there immediate freedom from past habits or has there been a gradual change?

Read Exodus 14:1–31

1 What were the difficulties the Israelites faced that made their situation an impossible one?

2 It was only God who could save the Israelites. Divide the chapter and your group into three and have each group look at a particular passage for evidence of God's hand at work.

3 It is difficult for us to accept that God derives his glory from drowning the Egyptians (14:4,17–18). How can you live with this aspect of God's character? Have other parts of Scripture or biblical examples helped you?

4 Scan the chapter for references to Moses. Remember Moses wrote this account. What does the narrative tell you about him and how he understood the whole Exodus experience?

5 Brainstorm the difference freedom would make to the lives of these Israelites.

6 In what ways can you compare the Exodus experience to the ultimate rescue plan Jesus offers people today?

> *All that happened through the Passover lamb in Israel's experience happens now through Jesus in our experience. His sacrifice on the cross brings sinners to judgement, principalities and powers to destruction, those under sentence of death to redemption, the oppressed into freedom and its participants into membership of a consecrated people.*
>
> **Derek Tidball**

HOW DOES THIS **7** Just as freedom changed the lives of the Israelite slaves, how should God's deliverance affect every aspect of our lives? APPLY TO ME?

HOW DOES THIS · **APPLY TO ME**

8 'God alone is responsible for salvation' – do you agree?

a) How does that statement help you reflect on what happened in your own conversion experience?

b) What does this statement mean in terms of our evangelism efforts and strategies?

APPLY THIS TO · **MY CHURCH**

9 Exodus 14:14 says 'The Lord will fight for you; you need only to be still.' Often as Christians we find ourselves in situations that only the Lord can change and we need to learn to wait upon him. Spend sometime praying for the ones in your group or church who are facing these kinds of situations.

God is not looking for people who will work for him, so much as he is looking for people who will let him work for them.

John Piper

WORSHIP

As a group look at Moses' song of praise to God for salvation (Ex. 15:1–18). Pick out the words and phrases that reveal God acted on your behalf the same way he did in the salvation of the Israelites – praise him for his faithfulness! Individually, spend time acknowledging that even though God alone is responsible for our salvation, we still like to stay in control of our lives. What everyday needs and concerns do you need to present to him and say 'God alone is able...'

FOR NEXT WEEK

Recognising our dependence on God for salvation and life can be difficult. At times we also find it difficult to be inter-dependent as a church body. This exercise might help you see the joy of receiving from others. Write your name on a piece of paper and fold it up. Put all the names into a hat and each pick out a piece of paper. Keep the name you picked out a secret but do something special for that person this week. Perhaps cook them a meal, baby-sit their children or send them a note of encouragement.

ACTIVITY PAGE

The Exodus and crossing of the Red Sea points forward to Jesus' death on the cross – the ultimate rescue plan for all humanity. Just like the Israelites, people are still being saved and their lives transformed by Christ. But as our society becomes more secular, it becomes more and more difficult for the church to nurture these new Christians – people's backgrounds and knowledge of God is so varied. Imagine the following scenarios. Brainstorm how you could help these new believers. What approach would be best to help each of these individuals grow as a Christian?

▶ A young person who grew up in your church and went through the Sunday school has recently returned from University. He became a Christian in the last few months of his course and would like to know where he goes from here.

▶ An older person joins the Alpha/Christianity Explored course. She has a church background but the course challenges everything that she had understood about God and salvation. Although she has become a Christian, she still has many questions. How can you help her?

▶ A lady who comes to the Mother and Toddler Group has become a Christian through the witness of other church women. She is living with her partner and is heavily into New Age spirituality. How would you help her grow as a Christian?

WILDERNESS WANDERINGS
SERVING GOD IN DESERT PLACES

AIM: To see the 'desert times' as opportunities for God to work in us, and in the people we serve

We've heard the phrase 'Church would be great if it wasn't for the people!' At church we often serve with those going through difficult times – and this isn't unusual. Remember the Israelites had to spend time in the desert before they ever reached the Promised Land. The key, especially for leaders like Moses, is to see what God wants to teach us in these times.

> *The whole Israelite community set out from the Desert of Sin, travelling from place to place as the Lord commanded. They camped at Rephidim, but there was no water for the people to drink. So they quarrelled with Moses and said 'Give us water to drink.'*
>
> *Moses replied 'Why do you quarrel with me? Why do you put the Lord to the test?'*
>
> *But the people were thirsty for water there, and they grumbled against Moses. They said, 'Why did you bring us up out of Egypt to make us and our children and our livestock die of thirst?'*
>
> *Then Moses cried out to the Lord, 'What am I to do with these people? They are almost ready to stone me.'*
>
> *The Lord answered Moses, 'Walk on ahead of the people. Take with you some of the elders of Israel and take in your hand the staff with which you struck the Nile, and go. I will stand there before you by the rock at Horeb. Strike the rock, and water will come out of it for the people to drink.' So Moses did this in the sight of the elders of Israel. And he called the place Massah and Meribah because the Israelites quarrelled and because they tested the Lord saying, 'Is the Lord among us or not?'*

Exodus 17:1–7

TO SET THE SCENE

Have a tasting session! Have some bowls of shredded wheat or other similar cereal for your group to try. Then offer them some pavlova or other delicious dessert. Which takes more effort or is more difficult to eat? Which tastes nicest? Which one is best for you? Can you draw any spiritual lesson from this fun exercise?

Read Exodus 17:1-7

1 How had God prepared Moses for this period of his leadership? Look back at Exodus 2:21-22, 3:1.

2 Looking at Exodus 17:1-7, what was Moses' primary role during these years? What do we learn about how leaders should guide members of their congregations through desert times?

3 Brainstorm all the other problems Moses faced during the years in the desert. What do you think the main lesson he learnt was?

4 Why do you think the Lord allowed it to be so difficult for the Israelites to get food and water to drink (Ex. 15:22–17:7)?

5 Exodus 17:6 tells us that God was present and yet the Israelites were questioning 'Is the Lord among us or not?' Given all God had done, why did the Israelites ask this? Why do we ask this question when we're going through desert times?

The desert road is not about 'wilderness spirituality' – voluntary withdrawal into an empty place in order to meet God. It is about what you might call 'exile spirituality', about finding yourself somewhere you do not want to be and looking for God in that situation.

Alison Jacobs

6 For all God's greatness at the Red Sea, the grind of the desert made the Hebrews long for slavery again. What does the patience, protection, provision and presence of God for the Hebrew slaves in their wilderness tell us about what we should be looking for in ours?

> Somehow,
> in the midst of our tears, a gift is hidden.
>
> Somehow,
> in the midst of mourning, the first steps of the dance take place.
>
> Somehow,
> the cries that well up from our losses belong to the song of gratitude.
>
> **Henri Nouwen**

7 This generation of Israelites did not enter the Promised Land because of their disobedience (Num. 14). Are there any ways in which our attitudes and behaviour stop us getting God's best?

8 Viv Thomas argues that 'God does not always give us our first choice lifestyle. Sometimes we must make do with a second choice – a Christian maturity is to be found in coming to terms with the reality in which God has placed us.' Do you agree/disagree with his point of view? Explain your answer.

> I keep looking, God, for the dramatic moment when I can engage in a glorious sacrifice for the faith. You keep presenting me with daily opportunities for belief and obedience and hope. Help me to forget my dreams of melodrama, and accept the reality of your kingdom.
>
> **Eugene Peterson**

HOW DOES THIS APPLY TO ME

9 a) What do you do in your own spiritual walk to find hope in desert places?

b) What helps you press on despite the difficult times in Christian ministry and leadership?

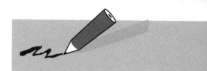

WORSHIP

The Israelites only seemed to worship God when life was going their way (compare Ex. 4:29–31 to 5:19–21). Be determined to worship God today no matter how your life is going or how you're feeling. Trust him, however long or barren the desert times may be. Worship God joyfully with songs of praise, listen to music, and encourage each other with Bible readings. Then bring your individual circumstances to God, remembering his promise in Exodus 17:6 'I will stand there before you.'

FURTHER STUDY

If you are going through a spiritually barren time try reading a new devotional book or missionary biography to inspire you. If you want to explore more about why God allows these times, try Philip Yancey's *Reaching for the Invisible God*.

FOR NEXT WEEK

Think of a person in your group or church who is going through a particular desert time. Phone them, take them out for coffee or see how you could help them practically, to remind them that not only is God close by but so are other Christian friends.

ACTIVITY PAGE

We all go through spiritual desert times – not even church leaders are immune! Sometimes God just seems distant and at other times our circumstances make us feel far from him. At these times we need encouragement but often we're too spiritually low to find it.

Prepare yourself a 'spiritual comfort package' that will cheer your heart the next time you face a barren time.

- Find and write out a favourite Bible passage that reminds you of God's faithfulness.
- Choose a favourite song or hymn and write out the words.
- Write down any prayers or quotes from Christian books that have been helpful to you.
- Write down answers to prayers you have got in the past year.
- Select a favourite Christian book.
- Write down the name of a friend that you would feel comfortable to talk and pray with – if no one comes to mind, take steps to build that kind of relationship with someone.

Pack all these items in a shoebox and only open when necessary!

THE TEN COMMANDMENTS
NEW LAWS FOR A NEW SOCIETY

 AIM: To live in a way which reflects God's rule in our lives

When Moses met with God on Mount Sinai, it wasn't simply to fall at his feet in worship, it wasn't only to declare his praises, it was to receive God's blueprint for this emerging nation. In the same way, God isn't interested only in our salvation but in how we live for him now.

> In the third month after the Israelites left Egypt – on the very day – they came to the Desert of Sinai. After they set out from Rephidim, they entered the Desert of Sinai, and Israel camped there in the desert in front of the mountain.
>
> Then Moses went up to God, and the Lord called to him from the mountain and said, 'This is what you are to say to the house of Jacob and what you are to say to the people of Israel: 'You yourselves have seen what I did to Egypt, and how I carried you on eagles' wings and brought you to myself. Now if you obey me fully and keep my covenant, then out of all nations you will be my treasured possession. Although the whole earth is mine, you will be for me a kingdom of priests and a holy nation.' These are the words you are to speak to the Israelites.

Exodus 19:1–6

TO SET THE SCENE
Brainstorm together some of the laws that have been passed nationally in the past six months. Which ones stick in your mind? What do these laws tell us about our society?

Read Exodus 19:1-25

1 a) What preparations had to be made for Moses to meet with God in Exodus 19?

b) What does this tell us about how we should approach God?

2 a) Receiving the Ten Commandments must have been one of the key moments of Moses' life. What was his role? Look also at Exodus 24.

b) In what ways does Moses' role compare with Jesus?

3 Scan Exodus 20–23. Why do you think the Mosaic Law covered such a diverse range of issues – from how the nation should behave to the positioning of fences and the treatment of donkeys?

> *It is a popular thought that the Israelites had to obey the law in order to be saved, but Exodus 20 is given to a people who have already been chosen and delivered. The law was given not to establish a close relationship but to perpetuate it.*
>
> **David Burnett**

4 The Ten Commandments and the Book of the Covenant covered issues such as idol worship and justice:

a) What are the idols of our day?

b) Why do you think God ensured the Israelite society made justice a priority?

c) What can we do to promote justice in our society?

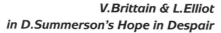

The United Nations estimates the cost of eradicating poverty at 1% of global income. Effective debt relief for the poorest countries would be even cheaper, with a price tag of $5.5 billion dollars – the cost of building Disneyland Paris.

V.Brittain & L.Elliot
in D.Summerson's Hope in Despair

5 Since we are New Covenant believers and we no longer live in a theocracy, to what extent should the Ten Commandments feature in our lives?

6 Look at Exodus 24. What did the Israelites do to confirm the covenant? In terms of approaching God, which elements have been abandoned, which remain the same, and why?

7 How can we as Christians live in a way that reflects God's rule in our lives?

8 The Israelites were meant to be a model to the other nations. What are the top five values or principles your church is modelling to the surrounding community? Be honest!

WORSHIP

Use your answers from question 6 to thank God for the unique access we, as the new people of God, have to him. As individuals, think whether there is anything hindering you from saying with the Israelites 'Everything the Lord has said we will do' (Ex. 24:3). Is there anything you need to give up in order to give God central place in your life? Is there an attitude you need to get rid of, a habit that is not God-honouring, or a persistent sin in your life?

FURTHER STUDY

If you want to look at the Commandments in more detail there is a book and video series available by J.John, entitled *Ten*.

FOR NEXT WEEK

Choose one of the Ten Commandments to meditate on this week. What does it mean in your particular context? Can you find practical ways of keeping and integrating it into your life this week?

ACTIVITY PAGE

The Ten Commandments and the Book of the Covenant introduce us to the values that are important to God, that are in fact part of his character. Look at the list of values below and note down how our contemporary society has distorted and limited them, and how we could express them as God intended. To help you get started the first two examples have been done for you.

Value	Today's Version	More Kingdom-Like Version
Loyalty	Only to our family	To all in our community
View of Person	Only the powerful matter	All people matter
Compassion	....	....
Repentance	....	....
Forgiveness	....	....
Sharing	....	....
Equality	....	....
Justice	....	....
Peacemaking	....	....

Discuss as a group how you could make these kingdom values more a part of who you are as individuals and as a church.

(Idea from Bryant L Myers, who produced the completed chart in *Walking with the Poor*, Orbis Books 1999)

CONSTRUCTION OF THE TABERNACLE
BUILDING GOD'S SANCTUARY

AIM: To see 'worship' not simply as a weekly event but as a lifestyle of obedience

Worship is a contentious issue in many of our churches. Unfortunately, when we're busy debating matters of style and content, we lose the awe the Israelites felt when God's presence dwelt among them for the first time; we lose sight of the privilege that God wants to be the centre of our lives, making a sanctuary in our hearts.

> *The Lord said to Moses, 'Tell the Israelites to bring me an offering. You are to receive the offering for me from each man whose heart prompts him to give. These are the offerings you are to receive from them: gold, silver and bronze; blue, purple and scarlet yarn and fine linen; goat hair; ram skins dyed red and hides of sea cows; acacia wood; olive oil for the light; spices for the anointing oil and for the fragrant incense; and onyx stones and other gems to be mounted on the ephod and breast piece.*
>
> *'Then have them make a sanctuary for me, and I will dwell among them. Make this tabernacle and all its furnishings exactly like the pattern I will show you.'*
>
> ***Exodus 25:1–9***

TO SET THE SCENE
Look through some popular magazines. Make a list of all the things that people 'worship'. What are the pursuits or beliefs people are devoted to, what do they idolise?

Read Exodus 26

1 How do you think God would define 'worship'? How do we define it?

> *To worship is to quicken the conscience by the holiness of God, to feed the mind with the truth of God, to purge the imagination by the beauty of God, to open the heart to the love of God, to devote the will to the purposes of God.*
>
> **William Temple**

2 'When you have brought the people out of Egypt, you will worship God on this mountain' (Ex. 3:12). God's intention has always been that his people worship him. What would the worship of God mean for these newly liberated slaves?

3 For Moses, the construction of the Tabernacle would have been one of the highlights of his career. Why do you think he listed God's instructions so precisely and virtually repeated them by recording their exact execution?

WHAT DOES SEARCH THE BIBLE SAY?

4 What do you learn about Moses' character from Exodus 40? How does his example challenge your preparation for worship?

WHAT DOES SEARCH THE BIBLE SAY?

5 Scan through Exodus 25–40. What principles do we learn about corporate worship from the concept and construction of the Tabernacle?

APPLY THIS TO MY CHURCH

6 What are your views on what corporate worship should look like, given these contemporary factors:

- ▶ There is little time for reflection in society
- ▶ There is a renewed interest in 'spirituality'
- ▶ We live in a media age
- ▶ We prize individuality above community

7 How does corporate worship on Sunday impact your individual worship throughout the rest of the week?

 HOW DOES THIS **8** How can we view doing the ordinary things of life as worship? What practical ways have you found to view the mundane **APPLY TO ME** as special to God?

> *I should like to speak of God not on the borders of life but at its centre…God is the 'beyond' in the midst of our life.*
>
> **Dietrich Bonhoeffer**

WORSHIP

We easily slip into patterns of corporate worship and each church develops its own style. Occasionally it is refreshing to experiment with a different style of worship: it helps us appreciate God more fully. If you are used to spontaneous exuberant worship, try using liturgy this week. Use some of the meditations from the Book of Common Prayer and spend some time in contemplation. If you are used to a more formal service, then perhaps read some poetry or write your own prayers. Try to be creative this week and use this opportunity to meet with God in a fresh way.

FOR NEXT WEEK

The Israelites were focused on getting to the Promised Land when God stopped them and told them to build the Tabernacle. When you are rushing to a pressing appointment this week or focused on all the tasks you have to do, make sure you take time to worship. Even viewing what you are doing as worship to God will alter your perspective!

FURTHER STUDY

If you would like to investigate this rich topic of worship more fully there are a number of books on the market. For example:

Jack Hayford – *Worship His Majesty,* Gospel Light

Graham Kendrick – *Worship,* Kingsway

John Piper – *Desiring God,* IVP

THE DEATH OF MOSES
EXAMINING HIS LEGACY

AIM: To persevere in serving God despite our failures

One thing guaranteed in life is failure. None of us like it, but we're all well acquainted with it! But failure doesn't need to signal an end to our service. God will take the sum of our lives, not just the times we've disappointed him, and provide us with a legacy he's proud of.

> *Then Moses climbed Mount Nebo from the plains of Moab to the top of Pisgah, across from Jericho. There the Lord showed him the whole land – from Gilead to Dan, all of Naphtali, the territory of Ephraim and Manasseh, all the land of Judah as far as the western sea, the Negev and the whole region of the Valley of Jericho, the City of Palms, as far as Zoar.*
>
> *And Moses the servant of the Lord died there in Moab, as the Lord had said. He buried him in Moab, in the valley opposite Beth Peor, but to this day no one knows where his grave is. Moses was a hundred and twenty years old when he died, yet his eyes were not weak, nor his strength gone.*
>
> *Since then, no prophet has risen in Israel like Moses, whom the Lord knew face to face, who did all those miraculous signs and wonders the Lord sent him to do in Egypt – to Pharaoh and all his officials and to the whole land. For no one has ever shown the mighty power or performed the awesome deeds that Moses did in the sight of Israel.*

Deuteronomy 34:1–3, 5–7, 10–12

TO SET THE SCENE

Brainstorm together your top five Britons. You may come up with many suggestions but decide on a top five and be able to defend your choices. What made these men and women great? What were the highlights of their careers? What part did failure have in their life?

Read Numbers 20:1–13

1 Why did simply striking the rock bar Moses from entry into the Promised Land?

2 What do you make of Moses' response to being barred from the Promised Land in Numbers 27:12–23? What does it tell us about Moses' heart and his leadership?

3 Imagine you're compiling Moses' curriculum vitae. On a flipchart list everything you know he accomplished. Then break into smaller groups, divide Numbers and Deuteronomy into smaller chunks, give each group a passage to scan. Is there anything else you can add to Moses' CV?

4 What is your favourite incident from the life of Moses? What spiritual lesson do you learn from it?

5 On a scale from 1–10 (1 being poor and 10 being exceptional) how would you rate Moses' overall performance as God's servant? Defend your answer!

6 How do you think God rated Moses' performance? Look at Deuteronomy 34: 1–12, Hebrews 3:2–6, 11:22–29, Matthew 17:3.

7 What does God's treatment of Moses' failure tell us about how he treats ours? (Think of God's judgement but also the commendation he gives Moses at the end of Deuteronomy for example.)

8 What three things (actions or attitudes) could stop you finishing the Christian life well? What practical action can you take to deal with these issues?

WORSHIP

Spend time asking God for forgiveness for past failures. As you think about your own weaknesses (question 8) consider the complementary strengths that Christ possesses. For example: if you are impatient, think about Christ being long-suffering. Spend time praying for each other that Christ would be more and more formed in you and that his strength would enable each member of the group to finish well.

FOR FUTURE WEEKS

'This is Your Life!' Just as you did the curriculum vitae for Moses, do one for yourself. Think through:

▶   What have been the high points of your Christian life?

▶   What ministry have you most enjoyed being involved in?

▶   What have been the low points?

▶   What have you learnt through your times of failure and disappointment?

▶   What would you most like to be remembered for?

Pray through these questions. Think particularly of how your answers to Question 8 make a real difference to the legacy you leave. When these familiar struggles surface again, make sure you meet with a prayer partner or friend to pray.

LEADERS' GUIDE

TO HELP YOU LEAD

You may have led a housegroup many times before or this may be your first time. Here is some advice on how to lead these studies:

▶ As a group leader, you don't have to be an expert or a lecturer. You are there to facilitate the learning of the group members – helping them to discover for themselves the wisdom in God's word. You should not be doing most of the talking or dishing out the answers, whatever the group expects from you!

▶ You do need to be aware of the group's dynamics, however. People can be quite quick to label themselves and each other in a group situation. One person might be seen as the expert, another the moaner who always has something to complain about. One person may be labelled as quiet and not be expected to contribute; another person may always jump in with something to say. Be aware of the different type of individuals in the group, but don't allow the labels to stick. You may need to encourage those who find it hard to get a word in, and quieten down those who always have something to say. Talk to members between sessions to find out how they feel about the group.

▶ The sessions are planned to try and engage every member in active learning. Of course you cannot force anyone to take part if they don't want to, but it won't be too easy to be a spectator. Activities that ask everyone to write down a word, or talk in twos, and then report back to the group are there for a reason. They give everyone space to think and form their opinion, even if not everyone voices it out loud.

▶ Do adapt the sessions for your group as you feel is appropriate. Some groups may know each other very well and will be prepared to talk at a deep level. New groups may take a bit of time to get to know each other before making themselves vulnerable, but encourage members to share their lives with each other.

▶ You probably won't be able to tackle all the questions in each session so decide in advance which ones are most appropriate to your group and situation.

▶ Encourage a number of replies to each question. The study is not about finding a single right answer, but about sharing experiences and thoughts in order to find out how to apply the Bible to peoples lives. When brainstorming, don't be too quick to evaluate the contributions. Write everything down and then have a look to see which suggestions are worth keeping.

▶ Similarly encourage everyone to ask questions, to voice doubts and to discuss difficulties. Some parts of the Bible are difficult to understand. Sometimes the

Christian faith throws up paradoxes. Painful things happen to us that make it difficult to see what God is doing. A housegroup should be a safe place to express all of this. If discussion doesn't resolve the issue, send everyone away to pray about it between sessions, and ask your minister for advice.

▶ Give yourself time in the week to read through the Bible passage and the questions. Read the Leaders' notes for the session, as different ways of presenting the questions are sometimes suggested. However, during the session don't be too quick to come in with the answer – sometimes people need space to think.

▶ Delegate as much as you like! The easiest activities to delegate are reading the text, and the worship sessions, but there are other ways to involve the group members. Giving people responsibility can help them own the session much more.

▶ Pray for group members by name, that God would meet with them during the week. Pray for the group session, for a constructive and helpful time. Ask the Lord to equip you as you lead the group.

THE STRUCTURE OF EACH SESSION

Feedback: find out what people remember from the previous session, or if they have been able to act during the week on what was discussed last time.

To set the scene: an activity or a question to get everyone thinking about the subject to be studied.

Bible reading: it's important actually to read the passage you are studying during the session. Ask someone to prepare this in advance or go around the group reading a verse or two each. Don't assume everyone will be happy to read out loud.

Questions and activities: adapt these as appropriate to your group. Some groups may enjoy a more activity-based approach; some may prefer just to discuss the questions. Try out some new things!

Worship: suggestions for creative worship and prayer are included, which give everyone an opportunity to respond to God, largely individually. Use these alongside singing or other group expressions of worship. Add a prayer time with opportunities to pray for group members and their families and friends.

For next week: this gives a specific task to do during the week, helping people to continue to think about or apply what they have learned.

For further study: suggestions are given for those people who want to study the themes further. These could be included in the housegroup if you feel it's appropriate and if there is time.

WHAT YOU NEED

A list of materials that are needed is printed at the start of each session in the Leaders' Guide. In addition you will probably need:

Bibles: the main Bible passage is printed in the book so that all the members can work from the same version. It will be useful to have other Bibles available, or to ask everyone to bring their own, so that other passages can be referred to.

Paper and Pens: for people who need more space than is in the book!

Flip chart: it is helpful to write down people's comments during a brainstorming session, so that none of the suggestions is lost. They may not be space for a proper flip chart in the average lounge, and having one may make it feel too much like a business meeting or lecture. Try getting someone to write on a big sheet of paper on the floor or coffee table, and then stick this up on the wall with blu-tack.

GROUND RULES

How do people know what is expected of them in a housegroup situation? Is it ever discussed, or do we just pick up clues from each other? You may find it helpful to discuss some ground rules for the housegroup at the start of this course, even if your group has been going a long time. This also gives you an opportunity to talk about how you, as the leader, see the group. Ask everyone to think about what they want to get out of the course. How do they want the group to work? What values do they want to be part of the group's experience; honesty, respect, confidentiality? How do they want their contributions to be treated? You could ask everyone to write down three ground rules on slips of paper and put them in a bowl. Pass the bowl around the group. Each person takes out a rule and reads it, and someone collates the list. Discuss the ground rules that have been suggested and come up with a top five. This method enables everyone to contribute fairly anonymously. Alternatively, if your group are all quite vocal, have a straight discussion about it!

NB – Not all questions in each session are covered, some are self-explanatory.

ICONS

 The aim of the session

 Engaging with the world

 Investigate what else the Bible says

 How does this apply to me?

 What about my church?

SESSION 1

TO SET THE SCENE

This is an icebreaker to help you get to know the others in your group better. This exercise should help you identify with Moses – the events and experiences from our past do impact us and God can use them to shape us for his service.

1   Salvation of humanity, gathering a people together who will truly know him and in response be totally committed to loving and worshipping him with their whole lives; fighting injustice and oppression, showing his power and glory.

2   A new Pharaoh who didn't remember Joseph came to power and he feared the rapid growth of the Israelites. So he oppressed them with hard physical labour and attempted to kill all the male children.

3   His mother recognised a special quality about him and Pharaoh's daughter spared his life.

4

The Palace years
   a)   He would not be overawed by Pharaoh, he'd be used to the culture and ritual of the palace court.
   b)   He would be well educated and therefore equal to facing Pharaoh.
   c)   Perhaps his privileged background would hinder his acceptance by his own people, the Israelites.

Murder of the Egyptian
   a)   He saw first-hand the plight of his people, he'd had to leave his home hastily just as the Israelites would have to.
   b)   He had a keen sense of justice and compassion. He was interested in his people and willing to intervene on their behalf.
   c)   He was hot-headed.

Desert-wanderings
   a)   Exiled, living in the desert as an alien and fugitive just like the Israelites would have to.
   b)   Kindness in helping the women at the well. The NIV says he 'rescued them'!
   c)   He was isolated from his people for a long time, out of circulation.

7   God 'heard, remembered, looked on, and was concerned' – he was not distant

but committed to the Israelites. The Exodus showed that God's sentiments led him to action. In the same way, through Christ, God has shown how much he loves and is committed to us.

WORSHIP

Give time for people to think through their part in God's mission. You may find people need to take time to talk and pray together in twos. But make sure you leave time to refocus the group on all that Christ has done for us.

DURING THE WEEK

Be willing to come back to the SWOT analysis in future weeks as people discover and are ready to share more about what they feel their part in God's plan is.

SESSION 2

MATERIALS

▶ Flipchart/A4 sheet of paper, pens, scissors
▶ CD or tape and music system

TO SET THE SCENE

Encourage each group member to be as creative as possible. Thinking about our passions, interests, and how God has wired us often is a clue to the specific 'calling' he has in mind for us. It's a fallacy that God will call us to do the very thing we don't want to do!

1   Holiness is being consecrated to God's service, wholly set aside for him. Holiness today can be displayed by an attitude of heart, in our values and priorities, by making Christ the central feature of our lives.

2   We may not have a spectacular call like Moses and our life may appear very mundane. The point is that in every situation we can fulfil God's greatest desire for us – holiness.

3   The introduction shows God hadn't forgot his covenant promise, hadn't neglected his people. He was faithful and passionate about them, not distant. Such an introduction gave Moses confidence and authority for his task.

4   God is the hero of the Old Testament, not Moses. Throughout this passage we can see him taking the initiative, carrying out his plan and being in control.

5   Faithful to his promises, eternal, forever the same, trustworthy, the ever-present God.

7   Knowing God's care, faithfulness and action on our behalf should encourage us to be obedient to all that he calls us to.

8   God gave Moses signs that the Exodus would happen, he sent Aaron to meet him, he told Moses how the plan would unfold and gave him more signs to convince the people. Clearly God knew Moses' character, where he would need encouragement and help but, at the same time he knew Moses was the man for the job because he was willing to put his own reputation on the line.

WORSHIP
Have a worship CD or tape ready to play.

DURING THE WEEK
Be aware of people in the group who have found the concept of 'calling' unsettling. Take time to pray and talk with them. They maybe locked into a work or life situation that they can't change – encourage them to be holy, even if life is difficult. If they are able to change their circumstances, encourage them to follow Jani Rubery's steps.

SESSION 3

MATERIALS NEEDED

▪ Bread and wine if you are going to share communion together.

TO SET THE SCENE

This exercise is not meant to embarrass anyone. We all break promises; either because we forget, we don't have enough time, or the situation changes and it's no longer wise to do so. We may have good reasons for not keeping our promises but God is so wise and sovereign that he never needs to go back on his word. He always keeps his promise and so is totally trustworthy.

2 God's glory was more fully seen in ten plagues rather than one – see Exodus 11:9, Romans 9:17.

4 Jesus defeated the penalty of sin but its presence is still here. Until heaven we will battle against sin in our own lives (the old sin nature), and in the world system. We need to be on guard against Satan's attacks (Eph. 6:10–18) and realise even though victory has been won we are still battling against 'principalities and powers'.

5

a) The lamb – was a perfect and spotless sacrifice pointing forward to Christ
b) Blood – indicates a substitute had taken place, the lamb had died instead of the eldest child, just as Jesus died in our place.
c) Bitter herbs – represented the bitterness of slavery
d) Bread without yeast – represented the haste with which the people left Egypt.

6 People can become slaves to debt, to sex, drugs, drink, work, materialism – and as Christians we can also be enslaved by these things as well as to fear, guilt, bitterness etc. We should remember people are also enslaved still by others, in countries such as the Sudan and also in the sex industries throughout the Third World.

7 Not only did the Israelites manage to flee, they also took with them the plunder the Egyptians gave them, as well as their herds.

8 God has given us many promises in the Bible. Look up Luke 12:27–31, Philippians 4:6–7, Matthew 28:19–20.

WORSHIP

In some cases it might be appropriate to mention to your minister about your wish to share communion together as a group. Adapt this section to your own church setting.

SESSION 4

MATERIALS

▶ A flipchart or large sheets of paper and pen for the different brainstorming questions

▶ Slips of paper, pens and a hat for the whole group for the 'For next week' exercise

TO SET THE SCENE

This is a time to get to know each other better as you share not only your conversion experience, but also what your life has been like, both before and after you became a Christian.

1 The Israelites were being pursued by a large, heavily armed force. They were also trapped between the Red Sea and the desert.

2 Throughout this account, God told Moses what the Israelites were to do. God knew what Pharaoh's strategy would be and planned to beat him (14:3); God was determined to bring glory to himself through this event and so hardened Pharaoh's heart (e.g. 14:4, 8); God's presence in the angel and pillar of cloud brought the Israelites protection (14:19–20); God divided the Red Sea to let the Israelites through but not the Egyptians (14:21–22, 26); God threw the Egyptian army into disarray (14:24–25).

3 We probably find this aspect of God's character so difficult to deal with because we don't fully appreciate our sinfulness or his sovereignty. For some reason, God is glorified through the judgement of the wicked and the salvation of the righteous (Rom. 9:19–21). At the same time God only judges those who harden their hearts to him like Pharaoh (Rom. 1:18–32).

4 Moses makes little mention of himself, preferring to portray God as the hero. He makes it clear that his own actions were given to him from God (e.g. 14:1–2, 26). We see his leadership as he talks to the Israelites (14:13–14) and also his honesty as he reveals God's slight exasperation with him (14:15).

5 The Israelites' situation will change from one of injustice to justice, from dependence to independence, from oppression to freedom in their own land, from slavery to becoming their own nation.

6 Both crossing the Red Sea and the cross were final, decisive events signalling a new start and new relationship with God; they are the only means of salvation; and they conferred a responsibility on the saved individuals to behave as the 'people of God'.

7 God's deliverance should affect who we live for, our priorities and values, our responsibilities as 'people of God'. We should have a change of master from Satan to God.

8

a) Even though we made a decision to accept Christ, it is true that we could do nothing to save ourselves from sin. God initiated and fulfilled the rescue plan.

b) God does all the saving but this doesn't negate our efforts in terms of prayer, building relationships with people and presenting the gospel effectively and in a relevant manner.

SESSION 5

MATERIALS NEEDED

▶ Plenty of spoons and bowls of shredded wheat (or other similar cereal) and delicious dessert if you're doing the Set the Scene exercise.

▶ Sound system and music for the Worship section.

TO SET THE SCENE

Hopefully this will be a pleasurable way to start your group this week! The idea is that the cereal, like desert times, is much more difficult to get through but is more beneficial for us than we realise. On the other hand the good times in life, like dessert, taste great but often aren't as good for our spiritual lives. In the difficult times we often make more spiritual progress because we have to trust more fully in God and we're at the end of our own resources.

1 Moses had already been an exile, an alien in a foreign land; he'd already spent time at the far side of the desert.

2 Moses was a mediator between the people and God. He listened to the people, he challenged them, and he tried to give them a right perspective on the situation and of God. Moses also cried out to the Lord for him to intervene, he explained what was happening, and was obedient to God's word to him. Our church leaders should try and be mediators in the same way as Moses.

3 Moses continued to face the people's cry for better conditions (Ex. 15:22–17:7), to deal with other leaders speaking against him (Num. 12), the people's lack of faithfulness to God (e.g. Ex. 32 and the Golden Calf incident), and with his own myriad of roles from legal representative to political leader. Your group could come up with many lessons that Moses must have learnt – to be obedient to God, to trust God wholly, that God cared and was so patient with his people etc.

4 Perhaps it was because he wanted the people to trust his timing, to learn that he would provide, and also perhaps because he wanted to test their obedience and commitment to him (e.g. Ex.16:4, 27–28).

5 The Israelites questioned God's presence because things were not going according to their plans: as far as they could see God wasn't working on their behalf. We feel the same as the Israelites; we've got short memories, often forgetting all God has done for us in the past.

6   God may not change our desert experience because he wants us to learn certain lessons but he will provide his protection and presence in those times – he wants us to rely on him rather than good feelings.

7   Often we do stay in the desert longer than we need, simply because we refuse to learn and be shaped according to God's will. Our obstinacy often prevents God from moving us forward into new phases of life.

SESSION 6

MATERIALS

▸ A supply of recent local and national newspapers for the To Set the Scene exercise.

TO SET THE SCENE

The laws of the land reflect the type of society we are and our leaders want us to become. Similarly, God's laws were designed to reflect the type of society he wanted the Israelites to become.

1

(a) Before God could be approached, the people had to be consecrated, their clothes washed, and there had to be boundary markers established so that they couldn't get too close to God, and they had to abstain from sexual relations. Essentially the Israelites had to purify themselves.

(b) As we have free access to God because of Jesus, we often approach God casually. But God demands the same degree of purity from us as he did of the Israelites, even if it is expressed in different ways! We should take care to confess our sins regularly, to approach him with reverence and to be wholehearted in our commitment to him.

2

a) Moses was the mediator between God and the people, he was the only one who could meet with God on the mountain, he conveyed God's requirements to them, he led the people in worship to God, and reminded them of God's word in the Book of the Covenant.

b) Moses pointed forward to Christ, the perfect mediator. Only Jesus could approach God's holiness and represent us before him. Only Jesus could tell us what God is like.

3 The laws are so diverse because the Israelites were starting from scratch; they had never had any laws before because they were under Pharaoh's rule. Also God sees no distinction between the sacred and the secular because he is the lawgiver for the whole of life. God wanted every area of their lives to measure up to his standard of justice.

a) Examples of contemporary idols are money, sex, power, freedom, career success, science, technology, and capitalism.
b) God wanted justice to be important to the Israelites because he is just and cares about injustice. It is part of his nature. He wanted his people to reflect his concern for justice in their dealings with each other, rather than to copy the way Pharaoh had treated them.
c) We can write to MPs, become involved with groups like Care for the Family, Evangelical Alliance etc. We can also get involved with local projects that look after the marginalised groups in society; homeless shelters, after school clubs for children who need special care etc.

The Israelites confirmed the covenant by declaring their obedience to God, building an altar, making a sacrifice and sprinkling animals' blood; but only Moses could approach God. Because of Jesus' sacrifice, we do not need to offer one. His shed blood means we can all enter God's presence. The altar we make is one in our own hearts – dedicating ourselves to obedience.

SESSION 7

MATERIALS

▶ Book of Common Prayer, paper and pens, candles etc – whatever you plan to use to make your worship time different to the style you usually use.

▶ Magazines for the To Set the Scene exercise.

TO SET THE SCENE

We often view 'worship' as a purely religious word but everybody worships. Society gives pre-eminence to many things – fitness, health, work, sex, marriage etc. Perhaps doing this exercise will fuel your worship of God even more because you'll appreciate again that he alone is worthy.

1 God views worship as our total allegiance and obedience to him, restoring an intimacy with us (Jn. 4:23). We often view worship as the songs that we sing on Sunday rather than the offering of our whole lives in response to all that God has done for us.

2 For the Israelites, worshipping God signalled their freedom, that their new master was God (Ex. 3:12, 4:23).

3 Moses showed his total obedience to God, he didn't take any initiative. The repetition of the instructions serves to underline how special it was to come into God's presence, his holiness was so great that care had to be taken with his dwelling, this was the first time God had dwelt with man like this. Hebrews 8:5 tell us the tabernacle had to be exact because it was a mirror of the one in heaven.

4 Again Moses' obedience is stressed. He was the only one authorised actually to erect the tabernacle – God's presence could not be taken lightly. This reminds us to get our hearts right before we come to worship services, that our everyday obedience is important if we want to meet with God.

5 The beauty, creativity and intricacy of the temple speak about the need for beauty in our worship, for people to use their creative gifts. The cycle of public worship reminded people of their responsibilities to God and we too need to be reminded. The tabernacle tells of God's presence with his people, and just as he was the centre of Israelite life, he wants to be centre of ours.

6 Encourage people to think as broadly as possible. Some answers could be to build times of contemplation into our services, to use the visual arts and multimedia to present the gospel, to emphasise community in practical ways.

7 However good a worship service is, its impact only continues if we spend time with God during the week, meditate on his word, and pray. The feelings may not necessarily last but each time we spend with the Lord, he feeds us and we grow spiritually, even if it's imperceptibly.

8 Come up with as many practical ideas as possible. For example, think of looking after the children, or meeting clients as doing it for Christ (Col. 3:17). Pray about the mundane items of the day, see the interruptions as appointments he brings into your life.

WORSHIP

Make sure you're not doing anything just for the sake of being different. Pray that God would make this a meaningful time for the group. Watch out for those who may find this change difficult to accept.

SESSION 8

MATERIALS

▶ Flipchart, paper and pens

TO SET THE SCENE

Discuss together what makes people 'great'. Even the 'greatest' Britons experienced failure but most of the time they learnt from it, used it constructively and did not see it as an end to their careers. Discuss how we, as Christians, experience and need to learn from our failures.

1 God said Moses had not trusted him enough, he should have known that a word would be sufficient to bring forth water. God's holiness was offended by Moses' hasty action. He showed a lack of respect for God in front of the people.

2 Moses' thought wasn't so much for himself as his people; he was keen to equip the next generation for leadership so they would be cared for.

3 Come up with as many incidents from Moses' life as possible. Include – establishing judges over the people of Israel; holding up his hands to ensure victory in war; the bronze serpent; seeing God's glory; the Ten Commandments; establishing the tabernacle; sending people in to explore Canaan; promoting Joshua as his successor.

6 Even though Moses had to live with the consequences of his failures, the Lord still regarded him highly. For example, he was God's prophet; God used him powerfully, showed him his face and buried him (Deut. 34). Moses was God's servant; he was a forerunner to Christ (Heb. 3). He was regarded as a hero of faith (Heb.11). He appeared at the transfiguration as representative of the Old Covenant (Mt. 17).

7 God held Moses accountable for his sins but he still used him mightily. Even at the end of his life, God commended him (Deut. 34). If we come back to God in humble repentance he will forgive our failings. While we have to face the consequences of our sins, they don't disqualify us from future service.

WORSHIP

As this is the last session in the series, allow people more time for prayer. Give them the opportunity to reflect and to rededicate themselves to God.

FURTHER INFORMATION

If you would like further information and resources, the following organisations may be of help. They will be able to tell you what is going on in your locality and how you can get involved:

THE EVANGELICAL ALLIANCE
186 Kennington Park Road
London
SE11 4BT
Tel 020 7207 2100
email info@eauk.org

CARE FOR THE FAMILY
PO Box 488
Cardiff
CF15 7YY
Tel 029 2081 0800
email: mail@cff.org.uk

FAITHWORKS
Tel 0207 450 9050
www.faithworkscampaign.org

OPEN DOORS
PO Box 6
Witney
Oxon
OX29 6WG
Tel 01993 885400
email: helpdesk@opendoorsuk.org

REBUILD
16 Kingston Road
London
SW19 1JZ
Tel 020 82395581
email info@rebuild.org.uk

TEARFUND
100 Church Rd
Teddington
TW11 8QE
Tel 020 8977 9144
www.tearfund.org

The story of Moses brings up many issues you might like to look at further. If you'd like to consider some of the issues in more depth, the Spring Harvest Study Guide for 2003 makes a great start. Here's a list of more specialised further reading.

Cover to Cover: God's Story – Phillip Greenslade & Selwyn Hughes, CWR
The Call – Os Guinness, Spring Harvest
Living on Purpose – Tom & Christine Sine, Monarch
Why Bother with Mission? – Stephen Gaukroger, IVP
More than a Job – Jani Rubery, Spring Harvest
The Message of the Cross – Derek Tidball, IVP
The Bondage Breaker – Dr Neil T. Anderson, Monarch
Second Choice: Embracing Life as it is – Viv Thomas, Paternoster Press
Desiring God – John Piper, IVP
The Expositor's Bible Commentary – Zondervan
NIV Application Commentary – Zondervan
Tyndale Commentary – IVP

NOTES

NOTES

NOTES